S: 1.0

D0793667

U.S. Navy Fighting Vessels

CAROL BALDWIN AND RON BALDWIN

Heinemann Library
Chicago, Illinois

© 2004 Heinemann Library,
a division of Reed Elsevier Inc.
Chicago, Illinois

Customer Service 888-454-2279

Visit our website at www.heinemannlibrary.com

Series design by Heinemann Library
Page layout by Malcolm Walker
Photo research by Bill Broyles
Printed and bound in China by
  WKT Company Limited.

08 07 06 05 04
10 9 8 7 6 5 4 3 2 1

Library of Congress Cataloging-in-Publication Data

Baldwin, Carol.
Know It! U.S. Navy Fighting Vessels / Carol and Ron
Baldwin.
  p. cm. (U.S. Armed Forces)
Summary: Provivdes an overview of the types of vessels used
by the United States Navy and their purposes.
Includes bibliographical references and index.
  ISBN 1-4034-4552-4 (HC), 1-4034-4558-3 (Pbk.)
1. United States. Navy--History--Juvenile literature.
2. United States. Navy--History. 3. Warships--United
States--Juvenile literature. 4. Warships--United States--
History--Juvenile literture. 5. Warships.
I. Title. II. U.S. Armed Forces (Series)
  VA61.B34 2004
  359.8'3'0973--dc22
                          2003023801

Produced for Heinemann Library by
White-Thomson Publishing Ltd
2/3 St Andrew's Place
Lewes UK   BN7 1UP

Acknowledgments
The author and publisher are grateful to the following for
permission to reproduce copyright material:

Title page, pp. 1, 3, 5B, 6–9, 11–15, 20, 21t, 22, 23b,
26–28, 29b, 30, 32b, 33, 35, 36, 38, 39, 40b, 42, 43 U.S.
Navy; pp. 4, 5t, 15b, 17, 18, 19, 23t, 24, 25, 29t, 31, 32t,
34, 37t, 41 Defense Visual Information Center; p. 10 Mark
Wilson/Getty Images; p. 16 Lockheed Martin Missiles &
Space/U.S. Navy; p. 21b National Archives and Records
Administration; p. 37b Alan Evans/Reuters/ Corbis; p. 40t
U.S. Navy/Reuters/Corbis

Cover courtesy of the U.S. Navy.

Every effort has been made to contact copyright holders of
any material reproduced in this book. Any omissions will be
rectified in subsequent printings if notice is given to the
publisher.

Special thanks to Lt. Col G.A. Lofaro for his review of
this book.

Note to the Reader: Some words are shown in
bold, **like this.** You can find out what they mean
by looking in the glossary.

Contents

The Navy Fleet

In the beginning

The United States Navy began in 1775 as the Continental Navy. In that year, a war started with Britain. The navy then was a tiny **fleet** of small, wooden ships. The British ships would not let ships into or out of our ports. At the end of the war, the British had to leave. About 60 ships served in the Continental Navy during the war. After the war ended in 1783, all the ships were sold. By 1785 our new nation had no navy.

In 1793 another war started in Europe. French and British navies raided American cargo ships. The United States built six new fighting ships. They bought more than about fifty other ships to protect our cargo ships. In 1798 the Navy Department was started.

This photo shows a ship built exactly like the 204-foot (62-meter) USS *Constitution*, which was one of six new fighting ships ordered built in 1794.

At the start of the 1991 Gulf War, the battleship USS *Wisconsin* hit Iraq with dozens of **missiles.**

Today's navy

Today our navy is the strongest in the world. It protects our country from enemy ships. It protects trading ships and ships that carry people. It also helps friendly countries fight their enemies.

Today's navy is a team of many vessels. **Carriers, cruisers, destroyers,** and submarines are the main fighting ships. Other navy ships aid them. Each kind of navy vessel has a special kind of job.

The cruiser USS *Cape St. George* and others like it fought in the Iraq war in 2003.

Battleships

Battleships used to be the navy's most powerful fighting ships. But today the navy has no battleships. The last battleship was the USS *Missouri*. It was taken out of service in 1992.

Aircraft Carriers

An **aircraft carrier** is a warship that has a **flight deck.** The flight deck lets aircraft take off and land. The navy's aircraft carriers are the world's largest ships. A carrier's deck is as wide as a football field. It is as long as 3¹/₂ football fields. Each carrier has as many as 85 aircraft on board.

Class name

The navy divides its ships into classes. Each class has a ship named for it. The Nimitz carrier class has nine ships with more planned for the future. One of them is the USS *Nimitz*. All the navy's carriers are about the same size. But there are some differences. Nimitz and Enterprise class carriers are nuclear powered. John F. Kennedy and Kitty Hawk carriers have steam engines.

The planes on the flight deck of the USS *Nimitz* get ready for the day's work during the Iraq war.

Naming Carriers

Most carriers are named for famous people. The USS *Nimitz* was named for Chester Nimitz, a famous admiral in World War II. Other carriers have been named for presidents, such as George Washington and Abraham Lincoln.

Below the flight deck

A carrier also has space to store aircraft below the flight deck. This area is called the **hangar deck.** Below the hangar deck are places for the crew to eat, sleep, and work. About 5,600 crew members live and work on a carrier. That is more people than live in many of our small cities. Because they are like small cities, each carrier has its own post office and zip code. Each carrier has a hospital, dentist office, barber shops, **mess halls,** chapels, and gyms. Crew members can also use e-mail and watch television.

Planes are stored in the hangar bay below the flight deck. Crew members work on the planes there. Huge elevators move planes between the hangar bay and the flight deck.

The arresting wire system can stop a 54,000-pound (24,500-kilogram) aircraft traveling 150 miles (241 kilometers) an hour in only two seconds.

Taking off and landing

The **flight deck** is not long enough for navy jets to make ordinary takeoffs or landings. So they get help from special machines. A carrier's **catapult** pushes a plane to get it up to high speeds in a short distance. If a plane is not moving fast enough, it will go off the end of the deck into the ocean.

To land, each plane needs a **tailhook.** This is just what it sounds like—a hook attached to the plane's tail. The pilot snags the tailhook on one of four cables, called **arresting wires,** on the deck to stop the plane.

Carrier Aircraft

- F/A-18 Hornets—fighter jets that attack enemy aircraft and ground targets
- E-2C Hawkeyes—planes that use radar to find enemy planes
- EA-6B Prowlers—planes that jam enemy radar and listen to enemy communication
- SH-60 Seahawks—helicopters that attack enemy submarines and rescue downed pilots

An SH-60 Seahawk takes off from a **carrier.**

Carriers during war

Aircraft carriers are sometimes moved into position before the battle begins. Five **carriers** took part in the war with Iraq. The USS *Harry S. Truman* sailed for the Mediterranean Sea on December 6, 2002. After it was at sea, its aircraft flew to the carrier. The USS *Nimitz*, USS *Theodore Roosevelt*, USS *Constellation*, and USS *Kitty Hawk* were also sent to the Persian Gulf or the Mediterranean Sea. Aircraft from carriers flew more than 7,000 missions during the war.

Gun Size

Gun sizes on ships are described in inches or millimeters. A 5-inch (127-millimeter) gun would fire a bullet 5 inches in diameter. That is about as big around as a large softball.

Carriers use **missiles** and big guns to defend themselves. Missiles can destroy enemy missiles and planes. They attack targets on land as well as at sea. Phalanx guns fire 20-millimeter shells very quickly.

A Sea Sparrow missile is being launched from the USS *Harry S Truman*. The missile can travel more than 2,600 miles (4,280 kilometers) an hour and reach targets nearly 35 miles (55 kilometers) away.

Cruisers

Cruisers are medium-sized warships. Some travel up to 35 miles (56 kilometers) an hour. The main job of cruisers is to protect **aircraft carriers** and support ships. They can attack enemy ships and targets on land. They protect troops landing on enemy beaches. Cruisers do their jobs with **missiles**, guns, and **torpedoes.**

Cruiser missiles

A cruiser has different kinds of missiles. Some missiles hit enemy ships. Other missiles attack land targets. Still others shoot down enemy aircraft. Cruisers also carry helicopters. They can search for enemy ships or submarines.

The USS *San Jacinto* fired 36 Tomahawk cruise missiles at Baghdad on March 22, 2003, the first night of the war with Iraq.

Tomahawk Cruise Missiles

Guided cruise missiles stay low over water or land to fool radar. Tomahawk cruise missiles can be fired from surface ships or submarines. They are used to hit targets on land. They can strike targets as far away as 1,500 miles (about 2,500 kilometers).

The Phalanx gun system on a cruiser is able to fire more than 3,000 bullets a minute at enemy aircraft or missiles.

Cruiser names

The Ticonderoga is the only class of cruisers. The navy has 27 cruisers. Each one has a crew of 364 people. A cruiser is 567 feet (173 meters) long. That is almost as long as two football fields.

Most cruisers are named after famous United States battles. They include the USS *Ticonderoga*, USS *Bunker Hill*, USS *Gettysburg*, and USS *Normandy*. One cruiser is named after Thomas S. Gates. He was the secretary of the navy from 1957 to 1959. He also served with the navy in World War II.

Destroyers

Destroyers patrol the sea around the fleet. They attack enemy planes, surface ships, and submarines before they can reach our ships. Arleigh Burke and Spruance are the two classes of destroyers. Both classes of destroyers attack with **missiles.** They also have Phalanx guns and 5-inch (12.7-cm) guns. Spruance class destroyers carry two Sea Hawk attack helicopters.

A destroyer's launcher can launch all kinds of missiles at different targets. The targets include ships, aircraft, submarines, and land targets.

The Spruance class destroyers were the first large navy ships to use **gas turbine engines** to move them through the water. Earlier ships used less powerful steam turbine engines.

Know It

The United States Navy has refitted some smaller destroyers as **frigates.** They changed some of the equipment on the ships in order to keep using them. Frigates are fast ships, but they do not have as many weapons as destroyers. They protect ship convoys and hunt for enemy submarines.

Crew members on the **bridge** control the navigation system. A ship's navigation system keeps the ship headed for the exact place it has been told to go.

Size and crew

There are 12 Spruance class destroyers and 39 Arleigh Burke class destroyers, which will increase to 47 in time. Ships of both classes are about as long as $1^1/_2$ football fields. Arleigh Burke destroyers have a crew of 323. Spruance ships have a crew of 382.

The First Destroyer

The USS *Bainbridge* was the navy's first destroyer. It had a crew of four officers and 69 sailors. The USS *Bainbridge* was built more than 100 years ago. It was first called a torpedo-boat destroyer because it was used to rid the sea of the enemy's deadly torpedo boats. Torpedo boats were small, fast boats that could dash in close to larger ships. They would fire their **torpedoes** and speed away. The name torpedo-boat destroyer was later shortened to destroyer.

Beneath the Waves

The United States Navy has three types of combat submarines. They patrol the world's waters unseen. They attack surface ships, other submarines, and land targets. They are the navy's largest fleet.

Attack submarines

Attack submarines destroy enemy surface ships and submarines. They also watch the waters near nations at war. Sometimes they land small teams of men for special missions. They are armed with MK-48 **torpedoes** and Tomahawk **missiles.** There are three classes of attack submarines with a total of 53 boats, and 4 more will be added.

The MK-48 Torpedo

The MK-48 is the navy's most powerful torpedo. Its warhead is packed with 650 pounds (292.5 kilograms) of explosives. It has a motor that moves it through the water. It can strike a target more than 5 miles (8 kilometers) away. All navy submarines carry MK-48 torpedoes.

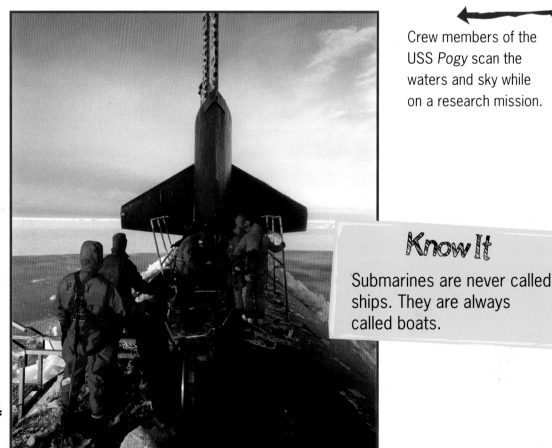

Crew members of the USS *Pogy* scan the waters and sky while on a research mission.

Know It

Submarines are never called ships. They are always called boats.

Guided missile submarines

The main job of guided missile submarines is to attack land targets. They do this with Tomahawk missiles. These submarines can carry up to 154 missiles. There are four boats of this Ohio class submarine. These submarines can also be used to land teams for special missions on enemy shores.

This drawing shows a nuclear-powered guided missile submarine. It can stay underwater for up to three months.

A submarine fires its missiles from bays such as this.

The Turtle

The first American submarine was called *Turtle*. It was built in 1775 during the American Revolution. A hand-driven propeller powered *Turtle*. To submerge, water was flooded into the submarine. This left the one-man crew in water up to his knees. He had to use a hand pump to remove the water before returning to the surface. *Turtle* was supposed to attach explosives to the bottom of British ships in New York Harbor. The idea did not work.

On guard—ballistic missile submarines

The main job of ballistic missile submarines is to keep other countries from starting a war with **nuclear weapons.** Other countries know what would happen if they did. They would be hit back hard by these submarines. A ballistic missile submarine carries 24 Trident nuclear missiles. No matter where an enemy country is, the Trident could hit it. The missile can hit targets as far away as 4,600 miles (7,400 kilometers). A submarine near North Carolina could send a missile to anywhere in Asia.

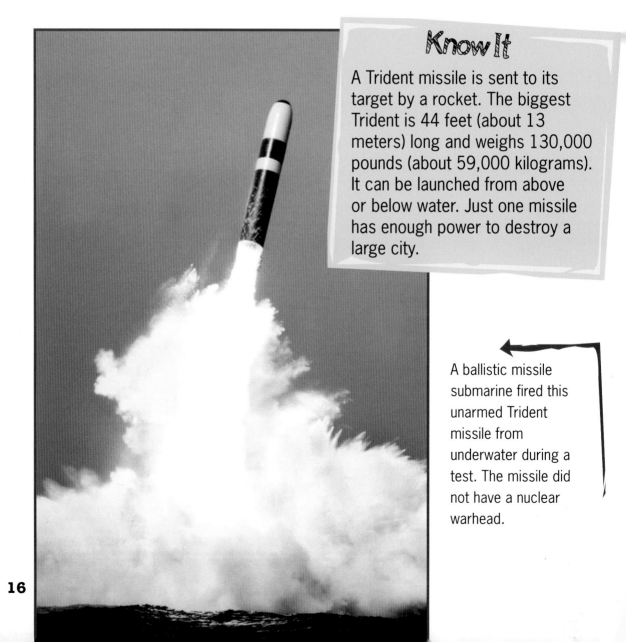

Know It

A Trident missile is sent to its target by a rocket. The biggest Trident is 44 feet (about 13 meters) long and weighs 130,000 pounds (about 59,000 kilograms). It can be launched from above or below water. Just one missile has enough power to destroy a large city.

A ballistic missile submarine fired this unarmed Trident missile from underwater during a test. The missile did not have a nuclear warhead.

Life on submarines

Living and working under the water is hard. The crew on a submarine needs fresh air and fresh water. They also need comfortable temperatures. Submarines have special ways of providing these things.

- To make fresh air, ocean water is pumped into a special machine. It separates the hydrogen and oxygen that make up water. The oxygen is used in the submarine. The hydrogen is put back into the ocean.

- A **distilling plant** makes fresh water. It brings in ocean water and removes the salt. The fresh water is stored in tanks.

- The water around a submarine is usually only about 39 °F (4 °C). The cold water takes heat from the submarine. So electric heaters are used to keep the air inside the submarine warm.

A submarine's torpedoes must be ready to fire with only a few minutes' notice.

Space is crowded on a submarine. There is little elbow room in the **mess hall.**

Attack submarines have a crew of more than 130. But they have only three shower stalls and one clothes washer and dryer to save space. Bunks are stacked three high.

Delivering the Goods

Amphibious assault ships

The United States Marine Corps is part of the U.S. Navy. **Amphibious** assault ships take marines and their gear close to an enemy's shore. Once there, the marines use landing craft and helicopters to get to a beach. Amphibious assault ships carry up to 1,900 marines. These ships defend themselves and the ships around them. They do this with **missiles**, attack planes, helicopters, Phalanx guns, and machine guns. The Wasp class has seven ships and the Tarawa has five ships.

Wasp Class

The navy's Wasp class amphibious assault ships are the largest in the world. They are almost as big as **aircraft carriers.** They are 844 feet (253 meters) long. Fully loaded they displace four times as much water as a navy **cruiser.** That's as much as 4,000 school buses weigh.

A landing craft leaves the amphibious assault ship USS *Nassau* with a load of marines.

Trucks that leave the Roll-on/Roll-off ship USNS *Pomeroy* using the ramp on the back are able to carry supplies to troops stationed inland.

Roll-on/Roll-off ships

These ships carry vehicles needed for war and for peaceful missions. They can carry 58 tanks and 48 other tracked vehicles. They can also carry more than 900 trucks. Huge doors with ramps open at the ship's rear and sides. This lets vehicles drive on or off. Two cranes help with the unloading. The ships also have a helicopter pad for emergency landings. The ships have a crew of between 26 and 45 civilians and up to 50 sailors.

Know It

The Military Sealift Command (MSC) operates the cargo and other support ships that supply U.S. Navy ships around the world. The crews of these ships are civilians. Some MSC ships also have some sailors to carry out special military jobs, such as supply operations.

Roll-on/Roll-off ships carried supplies for the Iraq war. Six ships carried **Humvees**, ammunition, helicopters, and food for the first wave of soldiers to fight in Iraq. The Roll-on/Roll-off ships have 380,000 square feet (35,302 square meters) of cargo space. That is almost as large as eight football fields. The biggest of these ships displaces as much water as 6,300 school buses.

Landing on the Beach

Landing craft carry troops and equipment from **amphibious** assault ships to beaches. The navy uses two types of landing craft.

Landing Craft, Air Cushioned (LCAC)

Air-cushioned landing craft are fast. With a full load, they can travel at 40 **knots** (46 miles or 73.6 kilometers an hour). They can transport up to 75 tons (68 metric tons) of cargo to the beach in one trip. They carry troops, weapons, tanks, and other equipment. Their speed means more troops can reach the shore in a shorter time.

Four large fans driven by **gas turbine engines** move the craft. The fans create a pocket of air under the craft. This air cushion lifts the craft off the surface of the water or beach. Other craft hit bottom in shallow water and must stop away from the beach.

The air cushion allows this landing craft to reach many more of the world's coastlines than other landing craft can.

This LCU is unloading marines at a port in Kuwait. The troops later traveled from Kuwait to Iraq to fight in the 2003 war.

Landing Craft, Mechanized and Utility (LCM and LCU)

These landing craft also move troops and equipment from assault ships to a beach. But they hit bottom in shallow water. So they stop before they reach the beach. Troops and equipment must splash the rest of the way in the water. The LCM craft has a ramp in front for loading and unloading. The LCU craft has ramps at both ends of the craft.

LCUs in WWII

Today's landing craft are much like the landing craft used during World War II (1941–1945). The main difference between the two is that today's craft have more space for the crews. The World War II landing craft carried up to 220 troops plus the crew. Today's landing craft carry between 80 and 200 troops.

During World War II, the United States used landing craft to land men and equipment on enemy beaches in Europe, Africa, Asia, and South Pacific Ocean islands. This operation was at Bougainville, a Solomon Island, in November 1943.

Here Come the Marines

Two kinds of navy ships are used to carry marines to war missions. They are the **Amphibious** Transport Dock (LPD) and the Dock Landing Ship (LSD).

Amphibious Transport Dock (LPD)

These ships carry troops, their equipment, and landing craft. They can carry up to 900 marines. The San Antonio class of LPD has five ships. There are eleven of the smaller Austin class ships. The ships are armed to defend themselves and their fighting cargo. They have missiles that can destroy enemy **missiles** and planes. They can carry combat helicopters or Osprey aircraft. They are also armed with Phalanx guns and machine guns.

Meeting the Needs

The LPD *San Antonio* has bunks that are high enough for a sailor or marine to sit up. This is something most ships do not have. It also has a learning resource center and electronics classroom.

The Osprey troop transport aircraft does not need a runway. Its propellers tilt so it can take off and land like a helicopter. Once in the air, the propellers move forward like other planes. The U.S. Congress is doubtful about what this aircraft can achieve, and the building program may not continue.

A Harpers Ferry class Dock Landing Ship can carry two of the large air-cushioned landing craft. A Whidbey Island class Dock Landing Ship can carry four.

Dock Landing Ship (LSD)

The Dock Landing Ship was built to carry air-cushioned landing craft and their crews. It can also carry other kinds of landing craft and helicopters to enemy shores. LSDs carry equipment and mechanics to repair all kinds of landing craft, too.

There are three classes of Dock Landing Ships with a total of 12 ships. All of the ships are armed with Phalanx guns and machine guns.

In 2002 the Dock Landing Ship USS *Germantown* took more than 300 marines and navy seabees and their landing craft to the Philippines. They built bridges and roads on Basilin Island. This was done to help Philippine Army troops. They are fighting terrorists on the island.

Almost all combat ships have machine guns for defense. A machine gun keeps firing bullets as long as the trigger is pressed. Dock Landing Ships carry MK 38 machine guns. These guns shoot 25-millimeter (1-inch) bullets.

When a marine **task force** is sent on a special mission, two kinds of ships meet them with supplies. Both kinds of ships are part of the Military Sealift Command.

Maritime prepositioning ships

Five of these ships carry enough to supply a task force of 17,000 marines for a month. They carry food, medicine, and a 200-bed field hospital. They bring tanks, weapons, ammunition, trucks, other vehicles, and fuel. There are three groups of maritime prepositioning ships. One group is based in the Mediterranean Sea. The second group is based in the Indian Ocean. The third group is based in the Pacific Ocean. Each group has five ships. They have civilian crews and navy technicians. Any of the groups can supply a marine task force.

A prepositioning ship can deliver thirty tanks to a marine task force.

Prepositioning ships have cranes that let them unload their own **cargo.**

Aviation logistic ships

The marine air force is kept in top condition by aviation logistic ships. They take care of the marines' planes and helicopters. They carry parts for all kinds of aircraft that the marines fly.

These ships have roll-on/roll-off decks that can take on planes. They can also take on aircraft when anchored offshore. The two aviation logistics ships are the SS *Wright* and the SS *Curtiss*. Each has a civilian crew of 37 plus 362 aircraft mechanics.

Shelters housing maintenance shops and equipment wait aboard the USS *Curtiss* to be used during the Persian Gulf War in 1991.

Service Stations

The navy cannot operate its ships and aircraft without fuel. Two kinds of Military Sealift Command (MSC) ships are fuel carriers.

Underway replenishment oilers

These ships stay with the fleet. They supply fuel for ships and aircraft whenever it is needed. They have stations on both sides of their decks to transfer fuel. They can carry 180,000 barrels of fuel. The Henry J. Kaiser is the only class of underway replenishment oilers. It has 14 ships. Each ship has a crew of 35 sailors and 89 civilians.

The USNS *Yukon* transfers jet fuel to the **amphibious** assault ship USS *Tarawa* during the Iraq war.

Know It

The amount of oil a tanker can carry is measured in barrels. One barrel is 31.5 gallons (119 liters) of oil. But the oil is not really carried in barrels. It is carried in huge tanks below the ship's deck.

A transport tanker refueling probe pulls away from a **destroyer** after completing the transfer of fuel.

Transport tankers

These tankers have many jobs. They work during war and peacetime. Transport tankers carry fuel for the United States Department of Defense. They take fuel to the National Science Foundation base in Antarctica. They travel to other civilian and military bases around the world. Each tanker can carry 257,000 barrels of fuel oil. These ships have double **hulls.** The outer hull is extra strong to protect against ice damage. Each of the five transport tankers has a crew of 23 civilians.

Compared to commercial oil tankers, transport tankers are small. A transport tanker is 615 feet (about 187 meters) long. The largest commercial oil tanker is almost three times as long.

Supplying Fighting Ships

Fuel ships are only part of the Military Sealift Command team. Many other kinds of ships supply ammunition, food, and equipment needed by the navy's fighting ships. These supply ships let the fighting ships do their jobs.

Delivering the firepower

Ammunition ships supply navy ships at sea. The crew connects cables between the two ships. Then, ammunition is loaded into a sling. The sling slides across the cable to the other ship. Ammunition ships also use Sea Knight helicopters to deliver ammunition. One ammunition ship, the USS *Mount Hood,* has a navy crew of 383. The other six ships have a crew of 125 civilians and 24 sailors. Some of the sailors fly the helicopters.

A Sea Knight helicopter gets ready to carry ammunition in a sling from an ammunition ship to an **aircraft carrier**.

Without combat stores ships, navy cooks would not be able to prepare the meals needed each day for the 5,600 people living and working on an aircraft carrier.

Food, clothing, and more

Six combat stores ships make sure that navy crews have food, clothing, and other things they need for daily living. They supply fresh, chilled, and frozen foods. They also supply bathroom items, clothes and shoes, and medicines. They also deliver mail.

The combat stores ships will bring whatever repair parts a fighting ship might need. Then the ship can be fixed while still at sea.

There are three Mars class and three Sirius class combat stores ships. Each ship has a crew of 49 sailors and up to 125 civilians. It also has two Sea Knight helicopters to deliver supplies.

Aircraft Carrier Daily Supplies

In a single day, the aircraft carrier *Kitty Hawk* uses:

- 9,600 to 12,000 eggs
- 400 to 600 gallons of milk
- 800 to 1,000 loaves of bread that are baked on the ship

Fast combat support ships

Fast combat support ships are like floating stores. They stay with **carrier battle groups.** They can carry 177,000 barrels of fuel. That is enough fuel to fill 600 large tanker trucks that you see on the roads. And they carry more than 2,000 tons (1,900 metric tons) of ammunition. That is enough to fill 80 very large dump trucks. They can also carry 750 tons (680 metric tons) of food. Smaller shuttle ships bring them all these required supplies. Then, the large, fast combat support ships take everything to carrier battle groups. This shortens the time needed to get fresh supplies to a carrier group.

The Supply class has one ship. The Sacramento class has four ships. All of them have Sea Knight helicopters to deliver food and ammunition to navy fighting ships. They are armed with Sea Sparrow **missiles,** Phalanx guns, and machine guns.

The USS *Sacramento* sends **cargo** over rigging lines to an **aircraft carrier.**

A fast sealift ship delivers trucks to a Roll-on/Roll-off ship for transfer to land.

Fast sealift ships

Fast sealift ships are the fastest cargo ships in the world. They travel as fast as 33 **knots** (38 miles or 61 kilometers an hour). They can travel from the United States to Europe in six days. Each of the eight ships is longer than three football fields. They quickly transport military equipment for all branches of the armed forces in an emergency. These large ships carry tanks, large wheeled vehicles, and helicopters. Together the eight ships can carry most of the equipment needed by an army division of 17,500 soldiers. To load and unload, they have ramps like those on Roll-on/Roll-off ships. They also have cranes and helicopters to help unload.

Auxiliary crane ships much like these delivered many of the supplies needed by our troops during the Iraq war.

Auxiliary crane ships

These ships are used to unload cargo onto shores that do not have proper docks. They have three cranes. Crane ships can unload their own cargo or cargo from another ship. There are ten ships in the one Keystone State class.

Saving Lives and Ships

The USNS *Mercy* is shown at sea during training.

Hospital ships

The USNS *Comfort* and the USNS *Mercy* are the two navy hospital ships. They go to the scene of fighting and take care of the wounded. Each ship has twelve operating rooms and a 1,000-bed hospital. They have all the equipment of a big hospital on land. Each has a landing deck for helicopters that bring in the wounded. They also have side ports. Boats can transfer wounded through these ports. A hospital ship has a crew of 61 civilians, 956 navy medical people, and 259 other navy crew members.

During the Iraq war in 2003, the USNS *Comfort* was stationed in the Arabian Sea. It gave medical care to wounded United States troops. It also cared for injured Iraqi civilians, such as this child, and enemy prisoners of war.

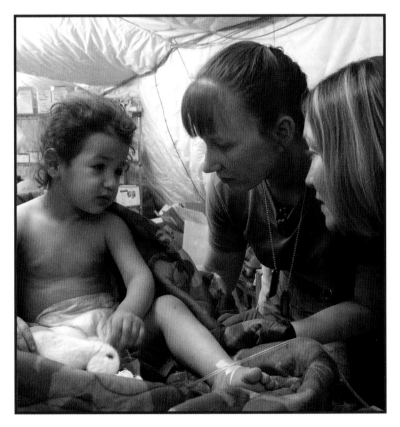

Help for ships in trouble

The navy's rescue and salvage ships are its lifeguards. They put out fires on other ships. They repair damaged ships and tow ships that cannot sail under their own power. These ships can also use tow wires to rescue a ship that is stranded on a beach. They have divers and huge cranes to bring sunken ships and downed airplanes to the surface. The navy has one class of rescue and salvage ships called the Safeguard class. The class has four ships, and each ship has a navy crew of 100.

If a ship is badly damaged, these ships rescue the crew of the damaged ship. They also give medical treatment to injured crew members.

Navy divers from a rescue and salvage ship often look for airplanes that crashed into the sea.

Command Ships

The commanders of the navy fighting team work from command ships. These are also called flagships. Admirals and other officers on these ships are in charge of the navy's **fleets.**

Command ships

These ships keep in contact with the Navy Department and ships and military bases all over the world. They always know where every ship in the fleet is. They tell each ship where to go and what to do. Command ships carry helicopters and are armed with rockets, Phalanx guns, and machine guns. They use air and surface **radar** to watch for enemy planes and ships. There are two command ships, the USS *La Salle* and the USS *Coronado*.

Know It

Air and surface radars find objects above the water's surface. Radar sends out a radio signal that bounces off an object and returns. This tells the radar operator an object's size, location, and speed.

Part of a command ship officer's job is to plan a fleet's training and combat missions.

Amphibious command ships

Amphibious command ships are the largest of the navy's command ships. They have a crew of 52 officers and 790 sailors. They carry enough food to feed their crews for 90 days. Their communication systems can send and receive messages from any place in the world. The two amphibious command ships are the USS *Blue Ridge* and the USS *Mount Whitney*. They carry helicopters and are armed with Phalanx guns and machine guns.

The USS *Blue Ridge* was built with a new design. It has fitness rooms, air conditioning, ship's stores, and large **mess halls.** These things help make life at sea more pleasant for the crew.

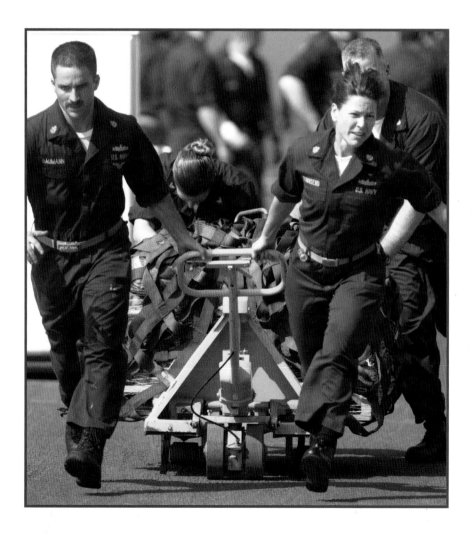

The USS *Mount Whitney* was the first fighting ship to let navy women work on board. Here, sailors move supplies the ship just received.

Mines Are Their Business

Mines are containers that hold explosives. They are placed under the surface of the water. They explode when ships run into them. Mines badly damage ships and can sink them.

The navy has 26 minesweepers. Their job is to clear a path in the water so a **fleet's** fighting ships can move through safely. They use navy divers, **sonar,** and video systems to find enemy mines. Then they send a remote-controlled device to the mine. The mine is usually exploded by remote control.

A minesweeper lowers a remotely operated vehicle into the water to search for mines.

When navy divers find a mine, they will tell the minesweeper its location.

Sonar

Sonar is used to find objects underwater. The sonar on minesweepers sends out sound waves into the water. The waves bounce off an object and return to the ship. This tells the sonar operator where the object is.

Mine-killing helicopters

Some navy ships carry helicopters that find and destroy mines. When a mine is found, the helicopter crew aims a laser beam at the mine. Then they fire a **missile**. The missile follows the laser beam to the mine and destroys it.

Navy Dolphins

The navy also trains dolphins to find mines. Dolphins use a kind of sonar called echolocation to locate objects in the water, so they are very good at finding mines. When it locates a mine, the dolphin swims close to it, but never touches the mine. The dolphin tows a package with its nose. It marks a mine by dropping the package near the mine. The package splits apart. An anchor stays on the bottom. A float is attached to the anchor by a line. Navy divers follow the line to the mine and take the mine apart.

Navy dolphins were part of the mine-hunting team clearing the harbor at Umm Qasr during the Iraq war.

37

Helping Out at Home

Patrol coastal ships

Navy ships have joined the United States Coast Guard in our homeland security mission. These ships help protect our ports and coastlines from attacks by terrorists. There are thirteen Cyclone class patrol ships. They are smaller than most Coast Guard ships. But they are very fast. They can travel at 40 miles (65 kilometers) an hour. Nine ships patrol our eastern coast. Four help guard our western coast. Any ship near our shores can be stopped and searched.

Cyclone class ships are also used to transport military Special Operations Forces groups. They are armed with **missiles,** grenade launchers, and machine guns.

Patrol coastal ships are named after winds and storms, such as *Hurricane, Tornado, Typhoon,* and *Whirlwind.* The USS *Firebolt* patrols the water near Yorktown, Virginia.

Fleet ocean tugs

Fleet ocean tugs are hardworking ships that do a lot of things. They tow damaged ships, recover downed aircraft, and bring up sunken ships. They have cranes and diving platforms. They can fight fires on other ships, go on rescue missions, and help clean the water of oil spills. They are also used to tow targets for a fighting ship's gun practice. Each of the six tugs has a crew of 16 civilians and 4 navy members.

The USS Cole Towed

The USNS *Catawba* tows the damaged destroyer USS *Cole* into open sea from the harbor at Aden, Yemen. Terrorists had blown a hole in the side of the *Cole's* hull. In deeper water, the *Cole* was placed aboard the Norwegian heavy transport ship M/V *Blue Marlin*. It was then taken to Mississippi for repairs.

USNS *Catawba* towed the USS *Cole* after it was attacked.

Underwater Workers

Deep Drone

The Deep Drone vehicle is operated by remote control. It needs no air tanks. It is used in deep ocean water to find sunken planes and ships. The Deep Drone can travel as deep as 7,200 feet (almost 2,200 meters). It has **sonar,** a still camera, and a video camera.

Deep Submergence Rescue Vehicle (DSRV)

The DSRV rescues crews on disabled submarines. It can be carried to where it is needed by aircraft, ship, or submarine. Once there, a crew of four takes the DSRV down to the disabled submarine. It attaches to the submarine's hatch and rescues its crew. It can take 24 people at a time to the surface.

When fitted with special lifting tools, the Deep Drone can bring objects weighing up to 3,200 pounds (1,450 kilograms) to the surface. That is about as much as a medium-sized car weighs. Here it has brought up the tail of an airplane.

The DSRV can reach a submarine in water as deep as 5,000 feet (1,524 meters). That's almost a mile, and it would take you about 15 minutes to walk that far.

Know It

DSRVs were developed after the USS *Thresher* submarine accident in 1963. The *Thresher* was practicing deep diving when things went wrong. At that time, rescue vehicles could not reach submarines in deep water. All the people on board the submarine died.

Mini Remotely Operated Vehicle (MROV)

The navy's two MROVs run on electricity. They use **sonar** to find objects in shallow water.

The sonar lets the operator know the size and depth of an object. MROVs have a regular camera. They also have a color television camera that makes videotapes. Each has a robot arm that can use simple tools.

Two navy technicians check an MROV before searching for 500-pound bombs lost in a Colorado lake crash in 1997.

SWISS

SWISS stands for Shallow Water Intermediate Search System. A SWISS is towed behind a ship at slow speed. It uses sonar to search the water below the surface. The sonar can find objects that are as deep as 5,000 feet (1,524 meters).

Secret Operations

Navy SEAL teams are part of the United States military's Special Operations Forces. SEAL stands for **SE**a, **A**ir, **L**and. These forces perform secret, and often dangerous, missions. The navy's Special Boat Units support SEAL teams on their missions.

Mark V Special Operations Craft (SOC)

The Mark V craft are very fast boats. They can travel 60 miles (97 kilometers) an hour. Their most important job is to carry SEAL combat swimmers. SEAL swimmers clear waters of mines and other underwater obstacles. This lets our fighting ships move in safely. Mark Vs can speed to where the SEAL team needs to be. Or they can be carried nearby on transport planes or ships. The boats are armed with **missiles,** grenade launchers, and machine guns. Each boat can carry sixteen SEALs.

The Mark V does not rise very high in the water, so it is very hard for enemy **radar** to track it.

Rigid Hull Inflatable Boats can move in water that is just a few feet deep. This means they are able to land a SEAL team almost anywhere.

Rigid Hull Inflatable Boats (RHIB)

This SEAL carrier is built to travel in high waves and strong winds. Their main job is to get SEAL teams to their mission area. RHIBs carry a crew of three and a SEAL team. Sometimes the SEAL team comes under attack. The RHIB crew must help defend them with the boat's machine guns. The RHIB crew patrols while they wait for the SEALS to finish their mission. Then they pick up the SEALs and speed them away when the mission is done. RHIBs can travel as far as 230 miles (370 kilometers).

SDV

SEALs also use small submarines to move underwater. The SEAL Delivery Vehicle (SDV) is a wet submarine. Water fills the inside of the submarine, so SEALS wear scuba gear as they travel in it. SEALs can use these submarines to reach mission sites in secret.

Another Look at the Navy's Major Fighting Vessels

Aircraft Carriers

Classes:	Nimitz
	Enterprise
	John F. Kennedy
	Kitty Hawk
Number of ships:	14
Attack aircraft:	75 to 85
Weapons:	Sea Sparrow missiles
	Phalanx guns
Crew:	Ships crew: 3, 200 to 3,350
	Pilots: 2,480

Cruisers

Classes:	Ticonderoga
Number of ships:	27
Aircraft:	4 helicopters
Weapons:	Standard missiles
	Vertical launch missiles
	Tomahawk missiles
	Torpedoes
	Phalanx guns
	5-inch guns
Crew:	364

Destroyers

Classes:	Arleigh Burke
	Spruance
Number of ships:	55
Aircraft:	Arleigh Burke—none
	Spruance—2 helicopters
Weapons:	Standard missiles
	Vertical launch missiles
	Tomahawk missiles
	Torpedoes
	Phalanx guns
	5-inch guns
Crew:	323 to 382

Submarines

Classes:	Ohio
	Virginia
	Seawolf
	Los Angeles
Number of boats:	75
Weapons:	Nuclear missiles
	Tomahawk missiles
	Torpedoes
Crew:	134 to 155

Glossary

aircraft carrier warship that has a deck where aircraft take off and land

amphibious can operate on land and in water

arresting wires cables on an aircraft carrier that stop a landing plane safely

battle group aircraft carrier and all the other ships that protect and support it during a war

bridge platform above the deck of a ship from which the officer in charge tells the ship where to go

cargo load of goods carried on a ship

carrier short way of saying **aircraft carrier**

catapult device for launching an airplane from the deck of a ship

convoy group of ships traveling together, usually with protection

cruiser medium-sized, fast warship armed with guided missiles, Phalanx guns, and torpedoes. Water displacement can be between 6,000 and 15,000 tons.

destroyer small, fast warship armed with 5-inch guns, Phalanx guns, depth charges, torpedoes, and guided missiles, usually used to protect larger ships

distilling plant machinery that turns seawater into freshwater

fleet group of warships under one command

flight deck deck where aircraft take off and land on a ship

frigate small warship equipped to destroy submarines

gas turbine engine engine that burns propane, kerosene, or jet fuel to make a hot gas that spins an engine's turbine

hangar deck deck where aircraft are stored on a carrier

hull outer covering of a ship, usually made of metal or wood

Humvees High Mobility Multipurpose Wheeled Vehicles. Its high ground clearance is designed to be used in all types of terrain and in all weather conditions.

knot measure of a ship's speed; a knot equals 1.1 miles or 1.852 kilometers an hour

mess hall place where a group of people eat together

missile rocket or bomb that is launched to destroy enemy planes, ships, or land targets

nuclear weapon object used in fighting that explodes and gives off deadly energy called radiation

radar instrument that uses radio waves to locate objects in the air, on land, or on the surface of water

sonar instrument that uses sound waves to locate objects underwater

submerge go below the surface of the water

tailhook hook attached to the tail of a plane that helps it stop after landing on an aircraft carrier

task force unit of troops assigned to a short-time mission

torpedo large, cigar-shaped missile that contains explosives and travels underwater by its own power; used to blow up enemy ships

water displacement weight of water pushed out of the way by a ship floating in water

More Books to Read

Abramovitz, Melissa. *On the Front Lines: The U.S. Navy at War.* Mankato, Minn.: Capstone High-Interest Books, 2002.

Burgan, Michael. *U.S. Navy Special Forces: Special Boat Units.* Mankato, Minn.: Capstone Books, 2000.

Gaines, Ann Graham. *The Navy in Action.* Berkeley Heights, New Jersey: Enslow Publishers, 2001.

Payan, Gregory and Alexander Guelke. *On Duty: Life on a Submarine.* Danbury, Conn.: Children's Press, 2000.

Presnall, Judith Janda. *Animals with Jobs: Navy Dolphins.* San Diego, Calif.: KidHaven Press, 2002.

Index